MW00333358

Jumpstarters for Vocabulary Building

Short Daily Warm-ups for the Classroom

By
CINDY BARDEN

COPYRIGHT © 2006 Mark Twain Media, Inc.

ISBN 1-58037-386-0

Printing No. CD-404054

Mark Twain Media, Inc., Publishers
Distributed by Carson-Dellosa Publishing Company, Inc.

The purchase of this book entitles the buyer to reproduce the student pages for classroom use only. Other permissions may be obtained by writing Mark Twain Media, Inc., Publishers.

All rights reserved. Printed in the United States of America.

Table of Contents

© Mark Twain Media, Inc., Publishers

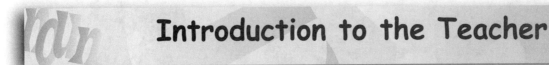

Introduction to the Teacher

Physical warm-ups help athletes prepare for more strenuous types of activity. Mental warm-ups help students prepare for the day's lesson while reviewing what they have previously learned.

The short warm-up activities presented in this book provide teachers and parents with activities to help students practice the skills they have already learned. Each page contains five warm-ups—one for each day of the school week. Used at the beginning of class, warm-ups help students focus on a vocabulary-related topic.

Types of Vocabulary Skill Activities

- **Using a Dictionary and Thesaurus:** Students explore a dictionary and thesaurus including definitions, guide words, parts of speech, antonyms, synonyms, and pronunciation guides.

- **Confusing Word Pairs:** Students learn how to correctly use word pairs that are often confused, such as *bought/brought* and *amount/number.*

- **Homophones: Words That Sound Alike:** Students confront the confusion of homophones, words that are pronounced the same, but spelled differently.

- **Homographs: Words With Multiple Meanings:** Students explore words with several very different meanings. Knowing more than one meaning for words allows students to understand better what they read and hear.

- **Synonyms and Antonyms:** Students learn synonyms, words that mean nearly the same, to expand their vocabularies. Learning antonyms, words that have opposite meanings, enables students to extend their word knowledge.

- **Compound Words:** A compound word combines two or more words to express a single idea. The meaning of the new word formed may be a very different meaning than the individual words used. Students also examine whether or not words should be used singly or as compounds words, depending on the context in which they are used.

- **Prefixes and Suffixes:** Students use knowledge of root words, prefixes, and suffixes to determine the meaning of unknown words. They discover that many words are built by adding both prefixes and suffixes, a process that helps students develop a larger vocabulary base.

- **Proper Nouns and Proper Adjectives:** With a reminder to capitalize, students take a tour around the world as they explore proper nouns and adjectives.

Introduction to the Teacher (cont.)

- **Numerical Words:** Students explore many common numerical words built from basic root words.

- **Acronyms:** Acronyms, words formed from the initials or other parts of several words, are everywhere.These activities help students learn acronyms ASAP.

- **Changing the Part of Speech of Words:** Changing nouns to adjectives, adverbs, and verbs; adjectives to adverbs; and verbs to nouns augments students' vocabulary base.

- **Words From Mythology:** Being able to identify mythological characters gives students a broader base for understanding references found in literature, movies, etc.

- **British English:** Students learn about British English and American English words for the same object.

- **Foreign Words and Phrases:** Students explore words and phrases with Latin, Greek, Spanish, French, and German origins that are commonly used in English. Recognizing the origins and meanings of frequently used foreign words in English enables students to understand and use these words accurately.

- **Idioms:** What people say is not exactly what they mean, as students learn when they interpret figurative language. Idioms are commonly used expressions that mean something different from the actual words.

Suggestions for Using This Book

- Copy and cut apart one page each week. Give students one warm-up activity each day at the beginning of class.

- Give each student a copy of the entire page to complete day by day. Students can keep the completed pages in a three-ring binder to use as a resource.

- Make transparencies of individual warm-ups and complete the activities as a group.

- Provide additional copies of warm-ups in your learning center for students to complete at random when they have a few extra minutes.

- Keep some warm-ups on hand to use as fill-ins when the class has a few extra minutes before lunch or dismissal.

Vocabulary Warm-ups: Using a Dictionary and Thesaurus

Name/Date _____

Using a Dictionary/Thesaurus 1

In your own words, briefly explain the difference between a dictionary and thesaurus.

_____
_____
_____
_____
_____

Name/Date _____

Using a Dictionary/Thesaurus 2

Write "D" for dictionary or "T" for thesaurus to indicate which would be better to use for each task.

___ 1. Determining the part of speech of a word

___ 2. Finding a synonym for a word

___ 3. Finding the exact definition for a word

___ 4. Finding an antonym for a word

Name/Date _____

Using a Dictionary/Thesaurus 3

In addition to definitions of words, write three other types of information found in a dictionary.

1. _____
2. _____
3. _____

Name/Date _____

Using a Dictionary/Thesaurus 4

Use a thesaurus. Write at least two synonyms for each word.

1. appearance: _____
2. say: _____
3. freedom: _____
4. look: _____

Name/Date _____

Using a Dictionary/Thesaurus 5

Use a dictionary. Circle the word in each row that is spelled correctly.

1.	philosophy	phylosophy	phylosophi	philosofy
2.	languige	language	lanugage	lanwage
3.	liberry	libery	libary	library
4.	scientest	sighentist	sciantist	scientist
5.	aperatus	apparatus	aperatis	aparatus

© Mark Twain Media, Inc., Publishers

Vocabulary Warm-ups: Using a Dictionary and Thesaurus

Name/Date _____

Using a Dictionary/Thesaurus 6

Use a dictionary to find the part of speech for each word. Then write a sentence using the word on your own paper. Some words may be more than one part of speech.

1. askance _____
2. particulate _____
3. palpable _____
4. illicit _____

Name/Date _____

Using a Dictionary/Thesaurus 7

Use a thesaurus to find at least two antonyms for each word.

1. success: _____
2. moist: _____
3. modern: _____
4. independent: _____

Name/Date _____

Using a Dictionary/Thesaurus 8

Use a dictionary. Circle the word in each row that is spelled correctly.

1. goverment   government   govormint   guvermint
2. unnecessary   unecessary   unnessicary   unecesary
3. insturmental   instermental   instirmental   instrumental
4. answer   anwser   anwsir   answar
5. thoro   thorogh   thorough   thorgh

Name/Date _____

Using a Dictionary/Thesaurus 9

Look up each word in a dictionary and write a definition for each word on your own paper.

1. postulate   2. hydrate
3. diatribe   4. peevish
5. brandish

Name/Date _____

Using a Dictionary/Thesaurus 10

Browse through your thesaurus. Select any word that has at least 10 synonyms and use that word as the title for a poem. Write a short poem using at least 10 synonyms for the word. Your poem can rhyme, but it does not have to rhyme. Write your poem on scrap paper, edit, and revise it. Rewrite it on good paper.

© Mark Twain Media, Inc., Publishers

4

Vocabulary Warm-ups:
Using a Dictionary and Thesaurus

Name/Date _____

Using a Dictionary/Thesaurus 11

Guide words can be found at the top of each page of entries in a dictionary. Explain how guide words help you use a dictionary.

_____

_____

_____

Name/Date _____

Using a Dictionary/Thesaurus 12

Many dictionaries use abbreviations, such as n. for noun or adj. for adjective. Find the chart for abbreviations in your dictionary. List four abbreviations used and what they mean.

1. _____   2. _____

3. _____   4. _____

Name/Date _____

Using a Dictionary/Thesaurus 13

Use software or the Internet to explore an online dictionary or thesaurus. On your own paper, name several ways it is like a printed book and several ways it is different.

DICTIONARY: [|_____] (ENTER)

THESAURUS: [|_____] (ENTER)

Name/Date _____

Using a Dictionary/Thesaurus 14

1. Where is the pronunciation key in your dictionary?

_____

2. How is it helpful to you? _____

_____

Name/Date _____

_____

Using a Dictionary/ Thesaurus 15

Open a dictionary to any page. Find three new words. Write the words and their definitions. Then, on your own paper, write a sentence using each word correctly.

1. _____

_____

_____

_____

_____

_____

2. _____

_____

_____

_____

_____

_____

_____

3. _____

_____

_____

_____

_____

_____

© Mark Twain Media, Inc., Publishers

Vocabulary Warm-ups: Confusing Word Pairs

Name/Date _____

Confusing Word Pairs 1

Bought is the past tense of *buy*.   **Brought** is the past tense of *bring*.

Complete the sentences using *bought* or *brought*.

1. Jill _____ the balloons to the party that she had _____ at the mall.
2. Sheila _____ a plate of cookies to the party.
3. Jason _____ soda at the grocery store.
4. Kevin _____ a friend to the party.

Name/Date _____

Confusing Word Pairs 2

Use a dictionary to write a short definition for each word. On another sheet of paper, write a sentence for each word.

1. choose: _____
2. chose: _____
3. loose: _____
4. lose: _____

Name/Date _____

Confusing Word Pairs 3

All together is a phrase meaning "everyone or everything in the same place."
Altogether is an adverb that means "entirely, completely, or in all."

Circle *altogether* or *all together* to complete the sentences correctly.
1. I ate (altogether/all together) too much pizza last night.
2. The team sat (altogether/all together) on the bench.

Name/Date _____

Confusing Word Pairs 4

Amount indicates "quantity, bulk, or mass."
Number indicates "units that can be counted."

Write *amount* or *number* on the blanks to complete these sentences correctly.
1. Can you guess the _____ of marbles in the jar?
2. What _____ of birdseed should we buy?
3. What a huge _____ of spaghetti you ate!

Name/Date _____

Confusing Word Pairs 5

On another sheet of paper, write sentences using each of these words correctly.

1. amount   2. number
3. altogether   4. all together
5. bought   6. brought

© Mark Twain Media, Inc., Publishers

Vocabulary Warm-ups: Confusing Word Pairs

Name/Date _____

_____

Confusing Word Pairs 6

Among is a preposition used when referring to more than two people or things.
Between is a preposition used when referring to only two people or things.

Write *between* or *among* to complete each phrase correctly.

1. _____ the two of us
2. _____ the trees of the forest
3. _____ the seven children
4. _____ the red one and the blue one
5. _____ a rock and a hard place
6. _____ all their friends

Name/Date _____

Confusing Word Pairs 7
Irritate means "to cause impatience, to provoke, or to annoy."
Aggravate means "to make a condition worse."

Circle the correct word to complete each sentence.
1. When the team lost, the coach was in a state of (aggravation/irritation).
2. Scratching (aggravated/irritated) his rash.
3. My father was (aggravated/irritated) by my low grade in math.

Name/Date _____

Confusing Word Pairs 8
Use a dictionary to write a short definition for each word. On another sheet of paper, write a sentence for each word.

1. borrow: _____
2. loan: _____
3. fewer: _____
4. less: _____

Name/Date _____

Confusing Word Pairs 9

Continual means "repeated often."
Continuous means "without a stop."
Circle the correct word to complete each sentence.
1. The (continual/continuous) sound of the surf lulls me to sleep at night.
2. The (continual/continuous) interruptions affected my concentration.

Name/Date _____

Confusing Word Pairs 10

On another sheet of paper, write sentences using each of these words correctly.

1. good	2. well	3. among
4. between	5. irritate	6. aggravate
7. continuous	8. continual	

Vocabulary Warm-ups: Confusing Word Pairs

Name/Date _____

Confusing Word Pairs 11

Effect means "to accomplish something or bring about a result."
Affect means "to act upon or influence."

Circle the correct word in each sentence.

1. The storm (affected/effected) our telephone service.
2. The (affect/effect) of the medication was amazing.
3. Will what I say have any (affect/effect) on you?

Name/Date _____

Confusing Word Pairs 12

Match these words with their definitions. Feel free to use a dictionary.

____ 1. advice   A. A machine or instrument
____ 2. advise   B. To think out, plan, or invent
____ 3. device   C. Information provided by someone
____ 4. devise   D. To provide information, especially when making a decision

Name/Date _____

Confusing Word Pairs 13

Good is an adjective used to modify a noun or pronoun.
        We enjoy good food. It is good to see you.
Well is an adverb that modifies verbs, adjectives, or other adverbs, or it is used as an adjective when it describes someone's health.
        He looked well. They were well dressed. She sang well.
Write *good* or *well* on the blanks to complete the sentences correctly.

1. She performed _____.
2. The pizza tasted _____.
3. These peppers are _____
4. He skates _____.
5. She made a _____ attempt to win.
6. Kent was not feeling _____.

Name/Date _____

Confusing Word Pairs 14

Accept means "to agree to something or to receive something."
Except means "to exclude or hold something apart."

Circle the correct word in each sentence.
1. Everyone agreed to the plan (accept/except) Herman.
2. Everyone who passed the test was (accepted/excepted) from homework yesterday.
3. Michael (accepted/excepted) his son's apology.

Name/Date _____

Confusing Word Pairs 15

On another sheet of paper, write sentences using each of these words correctly.

1. advice   2. advise
3. devise   4. device
5. borrow   6. lend
7. affect   8. effect

© Mark Twain Media, Inc., Publishers

Vocabulary Warm-ups:
Homophones: Words That Sound Alike

Name/Date _____

_____

Homophones 1

- **Homophones** are words that sound the same but have different meanings and spellings.

Principal means "a leader or chief"; "a sum of money that earns interest"; or "the most important."
Principle means "a truth, law, or moral outlook that governs how someone behaves."

Circle the correct word to complete each sentence.

1. He was a person of strong (principles/principals).
2. The (principles/principals) of nine schools met for lunch.
3. My advice is to spend the interest, but don't touch the (principle/principal).
4. Some scientific (principles/principals) are difficult to understand.
5. The (principle/principal) goal of the conference was to find a solution.

Name/Date _____

Homophones 2

Match these homophones with their definitions. Feel free to use a dictionary.

___ 1. stationary   A. not interested
___ 2. stationery   B. paper for writing letters
___ 3. board   C. associated with brides or weddings
___ 4. bored   D. motionless
___ 5. bridal   E. leather straps used to guide a horse
___ 6. bridle   F. lumber

Name/Date _____

Homophones 3

Use the words listed below to complete the sentences. Feel free to use a dictionary.

    reigns   **reins**   **straight**   **strait**

1. The king _____, but the queen holds the _____ of power.
2. If you travel _____ east by ship, you will reach the _____ of Gibraltar leading to the Mediterranean Sea.

Name/Date _____

Homophones 4

Write a brief definition for each word.

1. Capitol: _____

   _____

2. capital: _____

   _____

Name/Date _____

Homophones 5

On another sheet of paper, write sentences using each of these words.

1. capital   2. Capitol
3. stationary   4. stationery
5. bridal   6. bridle

© Mark Twain Media, Inc., Publishers

Vocabulary Warm-ups: Homophones: Words That Sound Alike

Name/Date _____

Homophones 6

Use the clues and a dictionary to answer the questions using the words listed.

pedal   peddle   residence   residents

1. I am a place where people live. What am I?
_____

2. I am part of a bicycle. What am I?
_____

3. I am a verb that means to sell. What am I?
_____

4. I am people who live in a specific place. What am I? _____

Name/Date _____

Homophones 7

Write the correct word from the list to complete each sentence. Feel free to use a dictionary.

peak   pique   peek

1. Please don't _____ while I hide the Easter eggs.

2. At the _____ of his fame, everyone knew his name.

3. Your idea does indeed _____ my interest!

Name/Date _____

Homophones 8

On your own paper, write a brief definition for each word and list its part of speech. Feel free to use a dictionary.

1. cite
2. site
3. sight
4. suite
5. sweet

Name/Date _____

Homophones 9

On your own paper, write a sentence using each word. Use a dictionary if you are unsure of the meaning of a word.

1. waste   2. waist
3. boulder   4. bolder
5. missal   6. missile
7. sleight   8. slight

Name/Date _____

Homophones 10

Match these homophones with their definitions. Feel free to use a dictionary.

_____ 1. bouillon   A. A snack served before a meal
_____ 2. bullion   B. A bone in the arm
_____ 3. canapé   C. Clear liquid made from boiling meat
_____ 4. canopy   D. Funny
_____ 5. humorous   E. A covering to block the sun
_____ 6. humerus   F. Gold bars

© Mark Twain Media, Inc., Publishers

Vocabulary Warm-ups: Homophones: Words That Sound Alike

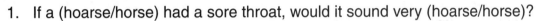

Name/Date _____

Homophones 11

Circle the correct word in each sentence. Use a dictionary to check your answers.

1. If a (hoarse/horse) had a sore throat, would it sound very (hoarse/horse)?
2. If you learn this (lessen/lesson) well, it will (lessen/lesson) the study time for your test.
3. Many (patience/patients) have very little (patience/patients) when they are ill.
4. The juniors (teamed/teemed) up to play basketball against the seniors.
5. The (beach/beech) (teamed/teemed) with seashells.

Name/Date _____

Homophones 12

Circle the correct words in each sentence. On your own paper, write a brief definition for each circled word.

1. Before the hot air balloon began its (ascent/assent), passengers had to sign an (ascent/assent) form.
2. Stop! Hit the (brake/break) before we (brake/break) the car!
3. On a (chili/chilly) day, a bowl of warm (chili/chilly) tastes terrific.

Name/Date _____

Homophones 13

Circle the correct words in the sentence, and name the parts of speech as they are used in the sentence. Use a dictionary to check your answers.

Emily found a lovely (piece/peace) of pink

_____

(choral/coral) that had washed up on the

_____

(beach/beech.) _____

Name/Date _____

Homophones 14

Circle the correct word in each sentence. Write a synonym for each circled word. Use a dictionary to check your answers.

1. The bride and groom walked hand in hand to the (altar/alter). _____
2. Sandy took a woodworking (coarse/course) at the Senior Center. _____

Name/Date _____

Homophones 15

On another sheet of paper, write sentences using each of these words correctly.

1. brake   2. ascent
3. assent   4. choral
5. hoarse   6. coarse
7. teem   8. lessen
9. alter   10. beech

© Mark Twain Media, Inc., Publishers

Vocabulary Warm-ups:
Homographs: Words With Multiple Meanings

Name/Date _____

Homographs 1

Use a dictionary to write a brief definition for the underlined word in each sentence that fits the context of the sentence.

1. Darryl will <u>graduate</u> from high school in June.

_____

_____

2. The <u>graduate</u> applied for several jobs last week.

_____

_____

3. The woman set her groceries on the <u>counter</u>.

_____

_____

4. My parents <u>countered</u> my request for a larger allowance.

_____

Name/Date _____

Homographs 2

On another sheet of paper, write sentences using these words as the part of speech listed.

1. *present* as a noun
2. *present* as a verb
3. *polish* as a verb
4. *Polish* as an adjective

Name/Date _____

Homographs 3

Use a dictionary to write a brief definition on another sheet of paper for the underlined word in each sentence that fits the context of the sentence.

1. Who will <u>conduct</u> the orchestra at tonight's concert?

2. Water <u>conducts</u> electricity.

3. His <u>conduct</u> during the crisis was admirable.

Name/Date _____

Homographs 4

Use a dictionary to write the part of speech for the underlined word in each sentence that fits the context of the sentence.

1. The chef uses beef <u>stock</u> in her soup. _____

2. The <u>stock</u> market rose 100 points on Friday.

_____

3. Ben worked for three hours to <u>stock</u> the shelves.

_____

Name/Date _____

Homographs 5

Use a dictionary to write a brief definition on another piece of paper for the underlined word in each sentence that fits the context of the sentence.

1. Will you <u>file</u> these reports today?
2. The students left in single <u>file</u>.
3. She used a <u>file</u> to smooth the edges of the wooden toy.
4. There is no information in my <u>file</u> about the missing wig.

© Mark Twain Media, Inc., Publishers

Vocabulary Warm-ups:
Homographs: Words With Multiple Meanings

Name/Date _____

Homographs 6

On another sheet of paper, write two short sentences for each word. Use the word as a verb in one sentence and as a noun in the second. Use a dictionary to check your answers.

1. crash	2. trap	3. station
4. smell	5. might	6. float

Name/Date _____

Homographs 7
Use a dictionary to write, on your own paper, the part of speech and a brief definition for the underlined word that fits the context of each sentence.

1. Please staple the pages together.
2. We need to go grocery shopping because we are out of many staples.

Name/Date _____

Homographs 8
Sometimes the pronunciation of a homograph changes, depending on whether it is a noun or a verb. Draw a slash (/) to divide the words below into syllables. Use an accent mark (') to show which syllable of the word is stressed for the part of speech listed.

1. *address* as a noun
2. *address* as a verb
3. *present* as a noun
4. *present* as a verb

Name/Date _____

Homographs 9

On another sheet of paper, write two brief definitions for each word that show completely different meanings for it.

1. tire	2. point	3. bend
4. bank	5. bright	6. fence

Name/Date _____

_____

Homographs 10

Write a word from the list to match each definition. Words will be used more than once.

ball	pack	stamp
shell	skate	

1. _____ a formal dance
2. _____ to skim across ice
3. _____ a deck of cards
4. _____ something found on a beach
5. _____ to fill a suitcase
6. _____ something people wear on their foot
7. _____ a child's round toy
8. _____ what you put on a letter
9. _____ what some people do with their feet when they are angry
10. _____ to take the outside covering off something, like peas or peanuts

Vocabulary Warm-ups:
Synonyms

Name/Date _____

Synonyms 1

Use a dictionary or thesaurus. Circle the words that are synonyms for the first word in each row.

1.	**circumspect**	cautious	round	prudent
2.	**incidental**	occasion	minor	significant
3.	**intricate**	complex	uncomplicated	difficult
4.	**gargantuan**	enormous	diminutive	mammoth
5.	**meticulous**	scrupulous	detailed	thorough

Name/Date _____

Synonyms 2

Use a dictionary or thesaurus. Cross out the word that is <u>not</u> a synonym for the first word in each row.

1. **deem**	show	believe
2. **numerous**	various	one
3. **chivalrous**	courteous	knight
4. **delusion**	illness	mirage
5. **exclusive**	unique	similar

Name/Date _____

Synonyms 3

Use a dictionary or thesaurus. Write two synonyms for each word.

1. belligerent: _____
2. auspicious: _____
3. authority: _____
4. antiquity: _____
5. unique: _____

Name/Date _____

Synonyms 4

Using a dictionary or thesaurus, match the words with their synonyms.

____	1. palpable	A. gigantic
____	2. peevish	B. harass
____	3. cavort	C. fretful
____	4. chivvy	D. dance
____	5. colossal	E. obvious

Name/Date _____

Synonyms 5

Use a dictionary or thesaurus. Write a synonym for each underlined word that matches the context of the sentence.

1. The horses drank from the water <u>trough</u>.
   _____

2. Please, turn down the <u>volume</u>.
   _____

3. Can't you be more <u>tolerant</u> of your little brother?
   _____

Vocabulary Warm-ups: Antonyms

Name/Date _____

_____

Antonyms 1

Using a dictionary or thesaurus, match the words with their antonyms.

_____ 1. sufficient

_____ 2. completed

_____ 3. complex

_____ 4. expand

_____ 5. glorious

A. shameful

B. scarcity

C. unfinished

D. uncomplicated

E. contract

Name/Date _____

Antonyms 2

Cross out the words that are not antonyms for the first word in each row. Use a dictionary or thesaurus to check your answers.

1. **abet**	aid	hinder	assist
2. **earnest**	fake	frivolous	sincere
3. **pugilistic**	warlike	friendly	hostile
4. **orate**	detailed	speak	silence
5. **paralyze**	mobile	still	motionless

Name/Date _____

Antonyms 3

Use a dictionary or thesaurus. Circle the words that are antonyms for the first word in each row.

1. **abundant**	scarce	plentiful	copious
2. **odious**	hateful	lovable	sweet
3. **monitor**	watch	check	ignore
4. **pulchritude**	beauty	humorous	ugliness
5. **eccentric**	odd	unusual	normal

Name/Date _____

Antonyms 4

Write two antonyms for each word. Use a dictionary or thesaurus.

1. accelerate _____

2. decisive _____

3. marine _____

4. laud _____

Name/Date _____

Antonyms 5

Using a dictionary or thesaurus, write an antonym for each underlined word that matches the context of the sentence.

1. That plan is not very practical. _____

2. We are practically neighbors. _____

3. He took a deep breath before he began the descent.

_____

4. Are there sufficient funds to cover expenses? _____

© Mark Twain Media, Inc., Publishers   15

Vocabulary Warm-ups: Compound Words

Name/Date _____

Compound Words 1

A **compound word** combines two or more words to express a single idea. Circle the compound words in each sentence. Draw lines to separate the compound words into single words.

1. A cupboard made of cardboard would not be good for storing teacups and tablespoons.
2. The redhead had an outstanding workout at the football field.

Name/Date _____

Compound Words 2

Use a dictionary to write a brief definition for each compound word. Write the definition on your own paper.

1. copperhead
2. runoff
3. horsepower
4. backspace
5. copyright
6. runway

Name/Date _____

Compound Words 3

Whether two words should be joined to make a compound word depends on the context in the sentence. Example: Any bird that is blue is a blue bird, but a bluebird is a specific type of bird. Underline the correct word or words in each sentence.

1. Do not let the (water fall/waterfall) on the carpet.
2. We sat by a beautiful (water fall/waterfall) and watched the sunset.
3. Is (any body/anybody) welcome to join the club?
4. Is there (any body/anybody) of water nearby in which to go fishing?
5. He wore (over alls/overalls) to keep his clothes clean.
6. She spilled paint (over all/overall) the papers.

Name/Date _____

Compound Words 4

On another sheet of paper, write a sentence using each compound word correctly.

1. earthwork
2. floodlights
3. network
4. overalls
5. standoff
6. freelance

Name/Date _____

Compound Words 5

Write two or more compound words that begin with each word listed.

1. every: _____
2. house: _____
3. week: _____
4. after: _____
5. back: _____

Vocabulary Warm-ups: Compound Words

Name/Date _____

Compound Words 6

Circle the compound words in each sentence. Draw lines to separate the compound words into single words.

1. I'll meet you in the stockroom soon. However, we cannot whitewash the staircase until this afternoon because I need a new paintbrush.
2. The stouthearted swordsman became an overprotective nursemaid for the princess.

Name/Date _____

Compound Words 7

Underline the correct word or words in each sentence.

1. The baby played with a fuzzy, (soft ball/softball) while her older brother went to his (soft ball/softball) game.
2. Will you help me? I could use a (second hand/secondhand).
3. I bought this hammer at the (second hand/secondhand) store.

Name/Date _____

Compound Words 8

Make a copy of a page from a novel or a magazine article. Circle all the compound words on the page.

Name/Date _____

Compound Words 9

On your own paper, write ten or more compound words that use each word listed below at the beginning or end of the new words. Use a dictionary if you need help.

1. under
2. day
3. up

Name/Date _____

Compound Words 10

Use a dictionary to write a brief definition for each compound word.

1. underdog: _____
2. downtrodden: _____
3. hourglass: _____
4. foreground: _____
5. lightheaded: _____
6. lopsided: _____

© Mark Twain Media, Inc., Publishers

Vocabulary Warm-ups:
Prefixes

Name/Date _____

Prefixes 1

A **prefix** is added to the beginning of a word and changes its meaning. Adding a prefix sometimes changes the spelling of the root word.

The prefixes "un-" and "non-" mean "not." Add the prefix "un-" or "non-" to each word to create a new word. Write a brief definition for each new word. Use a dictionary to check spelling and definitions.

1. likely _____ _____
2. profit _____ _____
3. sense _____ _____
4. tidy _____ _____

Name/Date _____

Prefixes 2

The prefixes "in-," "il-," "ir-," and "im-" all mean "not." Create new words by adding one of those prefixes to these words. Use a dictionary to check spelling.

1. logical _____
2. mature _____
3. active _____
4. literate _____
5. regular _____

Name/Date _____

Prefixes 3

Circle "T" for true or "F" for false. Use a dictionary to check your answers.

1. T F Prefixes can completely change the meaning of words.
2. T F *Hyperactive* and *hypoactive* have opposite meanings.
3. T F Prefixes are added to the beginning of a word.
4. T F The spelling of a root word may change when prefixes are added.

Name/Date _____

Prefixes 4

"Pre-" means "before"; "post-" means "after"; "dis-" means "to do the opposite"; and "re-" means "to do again." Match the words with their definitions.

____ 1. preseason   A. doubt
____ 2. distrust   B. after earning a degree
____ 3. postgraduate   C. before the regular season
____ 4. regroup   D. change around

Name/Date _____

Prefixes 5

On another sheet of paper, write sentences using any word that begins with each prefix listed. A dictionary can help you find words and their meanings.

1. un-   2. non-   3. dis-
4. post-   5. pre-   6. re-

© Mark Twain Media, Inc., Publishers

Vocabulary Warm-ups: Prefixes

Name/Date _____

Prefixes 6

Answer the following questions on your own paper.

1. How can knowing the meaning of a prefix help us figure out the meaning of a new word?
2. Use a dictionary to explain the difference in meaning between *interstate* and *intrastate*.

Name/Date _____

Prefixes 7

On another sheet of paper, write sentences using any word that begins with each prefix listed. A dictionary can help you find words and their meanings.

1. contra-   2. inter-   3. intra-
4. il-   5. de-   6. circum-

Name/Date _____

Prefixes 8

"Trans-" means "across"; "inter-" means "between"; and "sub-" means "below." Use a dictionary to write three or more words that begin with each prefix.

1. trans- _____

2. inter- _____

3. sub- _____

Name/Date _____

Prefixes 9

Circle "T" for true or "F" for false. Use a dictionary to check your answers.

1. T F *Inflatable* and *inflation* are synonyms.
2. T F *Inflate* and *deflate* are antonyms.
3. T F *Interstellar* means "between the seasons."
4. T F In the words *tricycle* and *triangle,* "tri-" means "three."
5. T F Prefixes always change nouns to verbs.

Name/Date _____

Prefixes 10

List a word for each prefix. Then give a brief definition for each new word. Use a dictionary to check your answers.

1. circum- (around)

_____
_____
_____

2. contra- (against)

_____
_____
_____

3. de- (down or from)

_____
_____
_____

4. tele- (far)

_____
_____
_____

5. retro- (backward)

_____
_____
_____

Vocabulary Warm-ups:
Suffixes

Name/Date _____

Suffixes 1

A **suffix** is added to the end of a word and changes its meaning. Adding a suffix sometimes changes the spelling of the root word.

The suffix "-less" means "without." The suffix "-some" means "full or like." Add the suffix "-less" or "-some" to each word. Write a brief definition for each new word. Use a dictionary to check answers.

1. home _____ _____

2. awe _____ _____

3. sense _____ _____

4. fear _____ _____

Name/Date _____

Suffixes 2

The suffix "-ment" means "the act of or state of something"; "-ible" and "-able" both mean "able to." Add one of these prefixes to the underlined root word in each sentence to fill in the blank.

1. Everyone <u>love</u>d the new puppy; it was so

   _____.

2. Dan didn't want to <u>retire</u> because he couldn't afford _____ yet.

3. Everyone knew Paul was _____ because he had a lot of common <u>sense</u>.

Name/Date _____

Suffixes 3

Circle "T" for true or "F" for false. Use a dictionary to check your answers.

1. T F   Suffixes can completely change the meaning of words.

2. T F   Suffixes are added to the beginning of a word.

3. T F   The spelling of a root word never changes when suffixes are added

---

Name/Date _____

Suffixes 4

Write a synonym for each word. Circle the root words. Use a dictionary to check your answers

1. critical _____

2. additional _____

3. gradually _____

4. professional _____

5. childish _____

6. profitable _____

Name/Date _____

Suffixes 5

On another sheet of paper, write sentences using any word that ends with each suffix listed.

1.   -able   2.   -ible   3.   -some

4.   -ish   5.   -ment   6.   -al

© Mark Twain Media, Inc., Publishers

Vocabulary Warm-ups: Suffixes

Name/Date _____

Suffixes 6

List a word for each suffix. Give a brief definition for each new word.

1. -ship _____

_____

2. -ance _____

_____

3. -ish _____

_____

Name/Date _____

Suffixes 7

Answer the following questions on your own paper.

1. How can knowing the meaning of a suffix help us figure out the meaning of a new word?

2. Use a dictionary to explain the difference in meaning between *democracy* and *demographic*.

Name/Date _____

Suffixes 8

Write the root words for each word in the parentheses. Then match the words with their definitions. Feel free to use a dictionary.

_____ 1. presentation (_____)

_____ 2. selection (_____)

_____ 3. exploration (_____)

_____ 4. appreciation (_____)

_____ 5. reflection (_____)

_____ 6. election (_____)

A. mirror image

B. discovery

C. process of voting for a candidate

D. choice

E. gratitude

F. demonstration

Name/Date _____

Suffixes 9

Use a dictionary to write five or more words that end with each suffix.

1. -dom _____

_____

2. -ic _____

_____

3. -ology _____

_____

Name/Date _____

Suffixes 10

Circle "T" for true or "F" for false. Use a dictionary to check your answers.

1. T F *Inflatable* and *inflation* are synonyms.

2. T F *Childish* and *childlike* are antonyms.

3. T F *Imitation, celebration,* and *conversation* are verbs.

4. T F In the words *biology, astrology,* and *geology,* "-ology" means "the study of."

5. T F Suffixes always change verbs to nouns.

© Mark Twain Media, Inc., Publishers

Vocabulary Warm-ups: Prefixes and Suffixes

Name/Date _____

_____

Prefixes and Suffixes 1

Many words combine a **root word** with a **prefix** and a **suffix**. For example, the word *disappointment* includes the prefix "dis-" and the suffix "-ment" added to the root word, *appoint*.

For each word, write the root word and a synonym for the root word.

1. untimely _____

   _____

2. impatiently _____

   _____

3. imperfectly _____

   _____

4. unhappily _____

   _____

5. unstoppable _____

   _____

Name/Date _____

Prefixes and Suffixes 2

Write the prefix, root word, and suffix for each word. Use a dictionary to check spelling.

	Prefix	Root word	Suffix
1. disappearance	_____	_____	_____
2. impossibility	_____	_____	_____
3. dishonorable	_____	_____	_____
4. insincerity	_____	_____	_____

Name/Date _____

Prefixes and Suffixes 3

For each word below, write the root words. Then, on your own paper, write a sentence using each word with the affixes.

1. discoloration _____

2. recreation _____

3. discontentment _____

4. unsuccessful _____

Name/Date _____

Prefixes and Suffixes 4

On your own paper, add a prefix and a suffix to each root word. Then write a short definition for each new word. Use a dictionary if you need help.

1. connect   2. manage   3. fortune

4. measure   5. appear

Name/Date _____

Prefixes and Suffixes 5

Use the root words given to write new words with a prefix and a suffix to complete the sentences.

1. appoint   Ty was _____ when he lost the race.

2. manage   Tori had a bad hair day; her hair was _____.

3. avoid   Growing old is _____.

© Mark Twain Media, Inc., Publishers

Vocabulary Warm-ups: Proper Nouns and Proper Adjectives

Name/Date _____

Proper Nouns and Proper Adjectives 1

Note: Always capitalize proper nouns and adjectives.

People in France speak French. In Germany, they speak German. Use a dictionary or other reference source to list the main language spoken by people in each country listed.

1. Czech Republic _____   2. Ukraine _____

3. The Netherlands _____   4. Greece _____

5. Republic of Azerbaijan _____

6. Republic of Finland _____

Name/Date _____

Proper Nouns and Proper Adjectives 2

Residents of Great Britain are called British. People who live in Thailand are Thai. Use a dictionary or other reference source to list the word used for residents of each country.

1. Republic of Hungary _____

2. Republic of Lithuania _____

3. Republic of Mozambique _____

4. Republic of Zimbabwe _____

Name/Date _____

Proper Nouns and Proper Adjectives 3

Use a dictionary or other reference source to find the correct spelling for each state.

1. Oaklahomma _____

2. Minesoda _____

3. Massashutes _____

4. Conneticut _____

5. Mississsippi _____

Name/Date _____

Proper Nouns and Proper Adjectives 4

Use a dictionary or other source to check the spelling of these countries. Rewrite the ones that are not spelled correctly.

1. Egpyt _____

2. Afghanistan _____

3. Bangladesh _____

4. Lebannon _____

5. Malaysia _____

6. Quwait _____

Name/Date _____

Proper Nouns and Proper Adjectives 5

Write two proper nouns for each category. Use a dictionary or other source to check the spelling.

1. U.S. cities _____

2. Presidents _____

3. Mountain ranges _____

4. Fictional characters _____

5. Athletes _____

6. Famous women _____

Vocabulary Warm-ups: Numerical Words

Name/Date _____

Numerical Words 1

Use a dictionary or other reference source to answer the following questions. Write the answers on your own paper.

1. Twins are two children born at the same time. What are quadruplets?
2. There are three musicians in a trio. How many are in a quintet?
3. How many notes are in an octave?
4. How many legs does a tripod have?
5. How many events are in a pentathlon?

Name/Date _____

Numerical Words 2

Use a dictionary or other reference source to answer the following questions. Write the answers on your own paper.

1. How many wheels does a unicycle have?
2. How many eyes does a Cyclops have?
3. How many events are in a decathlon?
4. How many languages does a person speak if he is bilingual?
5. How many bytes are in a megabyte?

Name/Date _____

Numerical Words 3

Use a dictionary or other reference source to answer the questions.

1. How many years are in a decade? _____
2. How many years are in a century? _____
3. How many years are in a millennium? _____
4. A centennial is an event that occurs once in 100 years. How often does a bicentennial event occur? _____
5. How often does a sesquicentennial event occur? _____

Name/Date _____

Numerical Words 4

Write three words not used elsewhere on this page that use "quad" or "oct" as part of the word. Write a sentence using each of the words.

1. _____
_____
2. _____
_____
3. _____
_____

Name/Date _____

Numerical Words 5

Write three words not used elsewhere on this page that use "tri" or "penta" as part of the word. Write a definition for each word.

1. _____
_____
2. _____
_____
3. _____
_____

© Mark Twain Media, Inc., Publishers

Vocabulary Warm-ups: Acronyms

Name/Date _____

Acronyms 1

Acronyms are words formed from the initials or other parts of several words. Usually, periods are not used in acronyms, and all letters are capitalized. Underline the acronyms. Use a dictionary to find the words these acronyms represent, and write those words on your own paper.

1. ID is required when cashing a check.
2. Tasha forgot her PIN number when she went to use the ATM.
3. At the B & B, I had OJ and a BLT, but Max wanted a PB & J.

Name/Date _____

Acronyms 2

Use a dictionary or other source to find the words these acronyms represent.

1. NIMBY _____
2. FYI _____
3. ASAP _____
4. COD _____
5. PC _____
6. UPC _____

Name/Date _____

Acronyms 3

Many terms related to time are also acronyms, such as AM and PM. AM stands for "ante meridian," which translates to "before noon." Write the words for the other time acronyms listed.

1. PM _____
2. EST _____
3. CST _____
4. PST _____
5. AD _____

Name/Date _____

Acronyms 4

On another sheet of paper, write sentences using each of these acronyms correctly. Use a dictionary to check the meanings.

1. ET   2. UFO   3. DNA
4. ISBN   5. IQ   6. PS
7. TGIF   8. RV

Name/Date _____

Acronyms 5

Some television series have used acronyms in their titles, such as *MASH* and *NYPD Blue*.

1. What does MASH mean? _____
2. What does NYPD mean? _____

In a detective show, you might hear the acronyms PI, MO, AKA, and SOP.

3. What does PI mean? _____
4. What does MO mean? _____
5. What does AKA mean? _____
6. What does SOP mean? _____

© Mark Twain Media, Inc., Publishers

Vocabulary Warm-ups:
Changing the Part of Speech of Words

Name/Date _____

Changing the Part of Speech of Words 1

Change these nouns to adjectives. Use a dictionary to check your answers.

1. beauty _____
2. fool _____
3. person _____
4. nation _____
5. style _____
6. music _____

Name/Date _____

Changing the Part of Speech of Words 2

Change these nouns to adverbs. Use a dictionary to check your answers.

1. fool _____
2. child _____
3. addition _____
4. fraction _____
5. truth _____
6. whole _____

Name/Date _____

Changing the Part of Speech of Words 3

Change each noun to any other part of speech. Write the part of speech of each new word. Use a dictionary to check your answers.

	New Word	Part of Speech
1. capital	_____	_____
2. storm	_____	_____
3. appearance	_____	_____
4. Russia	_____	_____
5. luck	_____	_____
6. industry	_____	_____

Name/Date _____

Changing the Part of Speech of Words 4

Change these verbs to nouns. Use a dictionary to check your answers.

1. complicate _____
2. collide _____
3. compute _____
4. officiate _____
5. confide _____
6. patronize _____

Name/Date _____

Changing the Part of Speech of Words 5

On your own paper, write sentences using each word in its verb form. Underline the verb form of the words.

1. introduction
2. confusion
3. arrival
4. entertainment

© Mark Twain Media, Inc., Publishers

Vocabulary Warm-ups:
Changing the Part of Speech of Words

Name/Date _____

Changing the Part of Speech of Words 6
Change each verb to a different part of speech. Write the part of speech of each new word.

	New Word	Part of Speech
1. believe	_____	_____
2. depend	_____	_____
3. use	_____	_____
4. circle	_____	_____

Name/Date _____

Changing the Part of Speech of Words 7
Change each adverb to a different part of speech. Write the part of speech of each new word.

	New Word	Part of Speech
1. frequently	_____	_____
2. rarely	_____	_____
3. considerably	_____	_____
4. methodically	_____	_____

Name/Date _____

Changing the Part of Speech of Words 8
On your own paper, write sentences using a verb form of each noun. Use a dictionary to check your answers.

1. instructor   2. administrator

3. abstinence   4. multiplication

5. knowledge   6. collector

Name/Date _____

Changing the Part of Speech of Words 9
How does changing the part of speech of words help you expand your vocabulary?

_____

_____

_____

Name/Date _____

Changing the Part of Speech of Words 10

Change these adjectives to adverbs. Use a dictionary to check your answers.

1. permanent

_____

2. obvious

_____

3. gradual

_____

4. second

_____

5. practical

_____

6. medical

_____

© Mark Twain Media, Inc., Publishers

Vocabulary Warm-ups: Words From Mythology

Name/Date _____

Words From Mythology 1

Write the word for each part human, part animal mythological creature below its picture. Use a dictionary or other reference source if you need help.

centaur   **sphinx**   **minotaur**   **mermaid**

1. _____   2. _____   3. _____   4. _____

Name/Date _____

Words From Mythology 2

Use a dictionary to match these mythological creatures with their definitions.

____ 1. satyr

____ 2. basilisk

____ 3. dryad

____ 4. naiad

A. a tree nymph

B. a water nymph

C. a reptilian creature that turned people to stone

D. a creature with the head of a man and body of a goat

Name/Date _____

Words From Mythology 3

Use a dictionary or other source to answer these questions. Write the answers on your own paper.

1. What three animals were combined in a chimera?
2. What could Pegasus do that a normal horse could not do?
3. How long was a phoenix said to live?
4. In what country's mythology would you find tales of genies?
5. What is an alternate spelling for genie?

Name/Date _____

Words From Mythology 4

Use a dictionary or other source to describe each of these mythological creatures. Write your answers on another sheet of paper.

1. Roc
2. Cerberus
3. Selkie
4. Salamander
5. Griffin

Name/Date _____

Words From Mythology 5

Use a dictionary or other source to complete the following. Use your own paper.

1. What country is famous for leprechauns?
2. In which country did the gods Ra and Osiris originate?
3. In what country were Vishnu, Brahma, and Shiva honored?
4. When a banshee wailed, what did it mean?
5. An ankh symbolized life in ancient Egypt. Draw an ankh.

© Mark Twain Media, Inc., Publishers

Vocabulary Warm-ups:
Classifying Words

Name/Date _____

Classifying Words 1

Circle the words from the list below that are mammals. Use a dictionary or other reference source to check your answers.

armadillo   earwig   echidna   halibut

javalina   moa   narwhal   ocelot

pangolin   tibia

Name/Date _____

Classifying Words 2

Cross out the words on the list below that are <u>not</u> types of documents. Use a dictionary to check your answers.

charter   constitution   contract

declaration   decree   honorarium

jurisdiction   sinecure   statute

tenure

Name/Date _____

Classifying Words 3

Rewrite these animal names next to the correct classification. Use a dictionary or other reference source to check your answers.

cicada   earwig   flounder   halibut   hellbender

manta ray   mud puppy   newt   praying mantis   salamander

walking stick   water strider   yellow-striped caecilian

Fish: _____

Insects: _____

Amphibians: _____

Name/Date _____

Classifying Words 4

Use a dictionary or other reference source to determine if each term refers to water or land. Write "W" for water or "L" for land in the blanks.

_____ 1. strait   _____ 2. isthmus

_____ 3. peninsula   _____ 4. gulf

_____ 5. estuary   _____ 6. delta

_____ 7. fjord   _____ 8. billabong

_____ 9. channel   _____ 10. mesa

Name/Date _____

Classifying Words 5

These words are classified as figures of speech. Use a dictionary to write a brief definition for each one and give an example. Write your answers on another sheet of paper.

1. hyperbole   2. metaphor

3. simile   4. onomatopoeia

© Mark Twain Media, Inc., Publishers

Vocabulary Warm-ups: Classifying Words

Name/Date _____

Classifying Words 6

Match the words from the list to the definitions. Use a dictionary to check your answers.

A. ichthyologist   **B. aviary**   **C. herpetologist**
D. apiary   **E. entomologist**

1. You would find many birds here: ____
2. The insects that live here make lots of honey: ____
3. A specialist in reptiles and amphibians: ____
4. One who specializes in the study of fish: ____
5. One who studies insects: ____

Name/Date _____

Classifying Words 7

Cross out the words on the list that are <u>not</u> birds. Use a dictionary or other reference source to check your answers.

barracuda   yellow jacket   emu   kiwi
fibula   finch
kookaburra   quetzal
egret   marlin

Name/Date _____

Classifying Words 8

Use a dictionary to match these types of doctors with their specialties.

____   1. dermatologist   A. eyes
____   2. obstetrician   B. young children
____   3. oncologist   C. delivering babies
____   4. pediatrician   D. nervous system
____   5. neurologist   E. cancer
____   6. ophthalmologist   F. skin

Name/Date _____

Classifying Words 9

Use a dictionary to fill in the blanks.

1. Geology is the study of _____.
2. Botany is the study of _____.
3. Anemology is the study of _____.
4. Meteorology is the study of _____.
5. Lexicology is the study of _____.
6. Cetology is the study of _____.

Name/Date _____

Classifying Words 10

Use a dictionary to write a brief definition for each math term. Be sure to use the mathematical definitions.

1. octothorpe: _____
2. radical: _____
3. googol: _____
4. hexagram: _____
5. octahedron: _____
6. protractor: _____

Vocabulary Warm-ups: British English

Name/Date _____

_____

British English 1

British English and **American English** sometimes seem like two different languages. In England, people post a letter to send it to someone, put a sticky plaster on a cut, and clean the windscreen when the windshield gets dirty.

Write the British English words from the list to match the common American English words. Use a dictionary if you get confused.

busker	**chemist**	**coach**
loo	**solicitor**	**whitener**

1. bathroom
   _____

2. bus
   _____

3. lawyer
   _____

4. non-dairy creamer
   _____

5. pharmacist
   _____

6. street entertainer
   _____

Name/Date _____

British English 2

Use a dictionary to write an American English synonym for each British English word.

1. Todd put the luggage in the car <u>boot</u>. _____

2. Would you like a <u>biscuit</u> with your tea? _____

3. At an English restaurant, you might order fish and <u>chips</u>.
   _____

4. The rugby team went to the <u>pitch</u> to practice. _____

Name/Date _____

British English 3

On another sheet of paper, write sentences using each of these British English words correctly. Use a dictionary to check your answers.

1. spanner
2. silencer
3. lorry
4. pram
5. porridge
6. dustbin

Name/Date _____

British English 4

Match the more familiar American English words with the British English words for the same objects. Use a dictionary to check your answers.

A. clothespin   **B. parka**   **C. underpass**
D. streetcar   **E. sherbet**   **F. elevator**

___ 1. anorak   ___ 2. tram   ___ 3. clothes peg
___ 4. lift   ___ 5. sorbet   ___ 6. subway

Name/Date _____

British English 5

Write the British English word for the underlined word in each sentence. Use a dictionary to check your answers.

petrol   **trolley**   **jumble**

1. The neighbors had a <u>rummage</u> sale in their garage.
   _____

2. Please fill the car with <u>gas</u>. _____

3. My <u>shopping cart</u> has a bent wheel. _____

© Mark Twain Media, Inc., Publishers

Vocabulary Warm-ups: Foreign Words and Phrases

Name/Date _____

Foreign Words and Phrases 1

Many English words come from Latin. For example, *dic* means "to say." *Predict, contradict,* and *edict* are common English words using *dic* as a root word. Use a dictionary to write on your own paper five or more English words for each Latin root word.

1. port - to carry
2. scrib or script - to write
3. ject - to throw
4. vert - to turn

Name/Date _____

Foreign Words and Phrases 2

Some foreign words are used in English without a change in spelling or meaning. Use a dictionary to write a short definition on your own paper for each German word also commonly used in English.

1. verboten
2. sauerkraut
3. doppelganger
4. kindergarten
5. gesundheit

Name/Date _____

Foreign Words and Phrases 3

Use a dictionary to match these Spanish words commonly used in English with their definitions.

_____ 1. sombrero   A. an enthusiastic person

_____ 2. siesta   B. a flour tortilla wrapped around meat, beans, or cheese

_____ 3. burrito   C. an afternoon nap

_____ 4. salsa   D. a spicy sauce

_____ 5. aficionado   E. a large-brimmed hat for blocking the sun

Name/Date _____

Foreign Words and Phrases 4

Use a dictionary to answer the questions.

1. What does the Spanish phrase *mano a mano* mean? _____

2. What does the Italian phrase *dolce vita* mean? _____

3. What does the Greek phrase *hoi polloi* mean? _____

Name/Date _____

Foreign Words and Phrases 5

Many English words use Greek root words. For example, *anthrop* means "human." *Anthropologist, misanthrope,* and *philanthropy* are English words using *anthrop* as a root word. Use a dictionary to find the definition for these words using the Greek *chron,* meaning "time." Write the definitions on your own paper.

1. chronicle   2. chronic

3. chronograph   4. synchronize

© Mark Twain Media, Inc., Publishers   32

Vocabulary Warm-ups: Foreign Words and Phrases

Name/Date _____

Latin Phrases 1

Read the translations for these Latin phrases commonly used in English. On another sheet of paper, write sentences using each phrase correctly. Use a dictionary if you need clarification.

1. *ad absurdum* - to the point of absurdity
2. *ad infinitum* - to infinity
3. *ad nauseam* - to a sickening degree
4. *bona fide* - in good faith; genuine
5. *carpe diem* - seize the day

bona fide

Name/Date _____

Latin Phrases 2

Use a dictionary or other source to match these Latin phrases with their meanings.

____ 1. *casus belli*   A. an act of the gods

____ 2. *caveat emptor*   B. after the fact

____ 3. *deus ex machina*   C. the cause of a war

____ 4. *ecce homo*   D. let the buyer beware

____ 5. *ex post facto*   E. behold the man

Name/Date _____

Latin Phrases 3

Underline the Latin phrase in each sentence. Rewrite the phrase in English so that it fits smoothly in the sentence. Write the answers on your own paper. Use a dictionary to check your answers.

1. While her mother was on vacation, Amy's grandmother acted *in loco parentis*.

2. "I can't stop now," Maria shouted, "I am *in medias res!*"

3. The archaeologist found the pottery *in situ*.

Name/Date _____

Latin Phrases 4

Use a dictionary or other reference source to answer these questions. Write the answers on another sheet of paper.

1. How much does a lawyer charge if she works *pro bono*?

2. Would you want to be a *persona non grata*? Why or why not?

3. Why were sailors terrified about sailing to *terra incognita*?

Name/Date _____

Latin Phrases 5

Use a dictionary or other source to find the meanings of these Latin phrases.

1. *mea culpa*: _____

_____

2. *quid pro quo*: _____

_____

3. *veni, vidi, vici*: _____

_____

© Mark Twain Media, Inc., Publishers

Vocabulary Warm-ups: Foreign Words and Phrases

Name/Date _____

French Phrases 1

Use a dictionary or other reference source to answer the following questions. Write the answers on your own paper.

1. *Beau geste* means a fine or noble gesture, often futile. What does *futile* mean?

2. If someone makes a *bon mot,* would it be polite to laugh? Why or why not?

3. Would you be happy if someone called you an *enfant terrible*? Why or why not?

Name/Date _____

French Phrases 2

Use a dictionary or other source to match these French phrases with their meanings.

____ 1. *coup de grâce*   A. the ability to say and do the correct thing
____ 2. *faux pas*   B. pen name
____ 3. *nom de plume*   C. finishing blow
____ 4. *savoir-faire*   D. a social blunder

Name/Date _____

French Phrases 3

Write a sentence using each of these French phrases on another sheet of paper. Use a dictionary or other source for clarification if needed.

1. *coup de grâce*   2. *faux pas*   3. *nom de plume*   4. *savoir-faire*

5. *carte blanche*   6. *beau geste*   7. *bon mot*   8. *enfant terrible*

Name/Date _____

French Phrases 4

In your opinion, why do you think many foreign phrases are commonly used in English?

_____

_____

Mark Twain was his nom de plume. What was his real name? _____

Name/Date _____

French Phrases 5

Use a dictionary or other source to find the meanings of these French phrases. Write the meanings on your own paper.

1. *bon vivant*   2. *cause célèbre*   3. *de rigueur*

4. *fait accompli*   5. *je ne sais quoi*   6. *carte blanche*

© Mark Twain Media, Inc., Publishers   34

Vocabulary Warm-ups: Idioms

Name/Date _____

Idioms 1

Idioms are commonly used expressions that mean something different from the actual words. For example, "Don't bite off more than you can chew" has nothing to do with eating. It means not to try something that's too difficult or advanced.

Underline the idiom in each sentence.

1. "No, I won't cheat on the test," Sara said. "It goes against my grain."
2. Jeremy was on cloud nine after he passed his vocabulary test.
3. Heather tried to knit a sweater, but she was all thumbs.
4. If you can't cut the mustard at practice, you won't make the team.
5. I hope you do well at your new job. I went out on a limb to get you hired.

Name/Date _____

Idioms 2

Use context clues to determine the meaning of each underlined idiom. Write the meanings on your own paper.

1. You can have anything you want for your birthday. The sky is the limit!
2. I can't understand our language arts assignment. It's Greek to me.
3. If you'd finish your term paper early, you wouldn't have to stay up all night and burn the midnight oil.

Name/Date _____

Idioms 3

Match the idioms with their meanings.

____ 1.	cross your fingers	A.	work hard
____ 2.	don't beat around the bush	B.	the last minute
____ 3.	add fuel to the fire	C.	hope for luck
____ 4.	keep your nose to the grindstone	D.	get to the point quickly
____ 5.	the eleventh hour	E.	make a situation worse

Name/Date _____

Idioms 4

Draw lines to match the two idioms that have similar meanings.

1. haste makes waste
2. all bark and no bite
3. down in the dumps
4. a shot in the dark
5. between a rock and a hard place

A. a real pussycat
B. out of the frying pan and into the fire
C. when pigs fly
D. Rome wasn't built in a day
E. feeling blue

Name/Date _____

Idioms 5

Write sentences on another sheet of paper using each of these idioms.

1. the apple of my eye
2. the sky is the limit
3. by the skin of your teeth
4. curiosity killed the cat
5. better late than never
6. let the cat out of the bag

© Mark Twain Media, Inc., Publishers

Vocabulary Warm-ups:
Idioms

Name/Date _____

Idioms 6

Write sentences on another sheet of paper using each of these idioms.

1. shoot the breeze
2. under the weather
3. a drop in the bucket
4. back to the drawing board
5. a chip on her shoulder
6. jump to conclusions

Name/Date _____

Idioms 7

Match the idioms with their meanings.

____ 1. as easy as pie
____ 2. sink or swim
____ 3. barking up the
          wrong tree
____ 4. in the doghouse
____ 5. a wolf in sheep's
          clothing

A. in trouble
B. asking the wrong
   person
C. simple
D. learn quickly, or
   end up in big
   trouble
E. a pretender

Name/Date _____

Idioms 8

On another sheet of paper, write the meaning of each idiom in your own words.

1. a slip of the tongue
2. elbow grease
3. shake a leg
4. put your best foot forward
5. in over your head
6. put your foot in your mouth

Name/Date _____

Idioms 9

Why do you think many people who learn English as a second language find idioms very difficult?

_____

_____

_____

_____

_____

Name/Date _____

Idioms 10

Fill in the blanks to finish each idiom correctly.

1. Appearances can be deceiving; you can't judge a book by its _____.

2. You won't change my mind, even if you argue until you're _____ in the face.

3. The judge was too lenient. He let Marshall go with only a slap on the _____.

4. Whenever I need help, I can always count on Shelby to lend a _____.

5. Don't fuss so much. You're making a _____ out of a molehill.

© Mark Twain Media, Inc., Publishers   36

Vocabulary Warm-ups: Answer Keys

Using a Dictionary and Thesaurus 1 (p. 3)
Answers will vary.

Using a Dictionary and Thesaurus 2 (p. 3)
1. D   2. T   3. D   4. T

Using a Dictionary and Thesaurus 3 (p. 3)
Answers will vary.

Using a Dictionary and Thesaurus 4 (p. 3)
Answers will vary. Possible answers are listed.
1. sight; show; scene; view; outlook
2. speak; utter; talk; state; declare
3. liberty; autonomy; independence; choice
4. see; stare; gaze; glance; spy

Using a Dictionary and Thesaurus 5 (p. 3)
1. philosophy   2. language
3. library   4. scientist
5. apparatus

Using a Dictionary and Thesaurus 6 (p. 4)
Sentences will vary.
1. askance: adverb
2. particulate: noun or adjective
3. palpable: adjective
4. illicit: adjective

Using a Dictionary and Thesaurus 7 (p. 4)
Answers will vary. Possible answers given.
1. failure; malfunction; collapse
2. dry; arid; parched
3. antique; old-fashioned; traditional
4. dependent; needy, reliant

Using a Dictionary and Thesaurus 8 (p. 4)
1. government   2. unnecessary
3. instrumental   4. answer
5. thorough

Using a Dictionary and Thesaurus 9 (p. 4)
1. postulate: to assume or suggest something is true
2. hydrate: to provide water in order to maintain a correct fluid balance

3. diatribe: a criticism, often bitter or accusing in nature
4. peevish: fretful, cross, or complaining
5. brandish: to wave something about, often in a threatening manner

Using a Dictionary and Thesaurus 10 (p. 4)
Answers will vary.

Using a Dictionary and Thesaurus 11, 12, 13, 14, 15 (p. 5)
Answers will vary.

Confusing Word Pairs 1 (p. 6)
1. brought; bought   2. brought
3. bought   4. brought

Confusing Word Pairs 2 (p. 6)
Sentences will vary.
1. choose: to select
2. chose: past tense of choose
3. loose: not tight
4. lose: to misplace something

Confusing Word Pairs 3 (p. 6)
1. altogether   2. all together

Confusing Word Pairs 4 (p. 6)
1. number   2. amount
3. amount

Confusing Word Pairs 5 (p. 6)
Answers will vary.

Confusing Word Pairs 6 (p. 7)
1. between   2. among
3. among   4. between
5. between   6. among

Confusing Word Pairs 7 (p. 7)
1. irritation   2. aggravated
3. irritated

© Mark Twain Media, Inc., Publishers

Confusing Word Pairs 8 (p. 7)
Sentences will vary.
1. borrow: to receive something with the intention of returning the same or an equivalent
2. loan: money or an item received in exchange for a promise to pay it back, usually with interest
3. Fewer is used with items or people that can be counted and is used with plural nouns.
4. Less indicates amount or degree and is used with singular nouns.

Confusing Word Pairs 9 (p. 7)
1. continuous   2. continual

Confusing Word Pairs 10 (p. 7)
Answers will vary.

Confusing Word Pairs 11 (p. 8)
1. affected   2. effect
3. effect

Confusing Word Pairs 12 (p. 8)
1. C   2. D   3. A   4. B

Confusing Word Pairs 13 (p. 8)
1. well   2. good
3. good   4. well
5. good   6. well

Confusing Word Pairs 14 (p. 8)
1. except   2. excepted
3. accepted

Confusing Word Pairs 15 (p. 8)
Answers will vary.

Homophones 1 (p. 9)
1. principles   2. principals
3. principal   4. principles
5. principal

Homophones 2 (p. 9)
1. D   2. B   3. F   4. A
5. C   6. E

Homophones 3 (p. 9)
1. reigns; reins   2. straight; strait

Homophones 4 (p. 9)
1. The government building in Washington, D.C.
2. A seat of government; money for investing; uppercase letter

Homophones 5 (p. 9)
Sentences will vary.

Homophones 6 (p. 10)
1. residence   2. pedal
3. peddle   4. residents

Homophones 7 (p. 10)
1. peek   2. peak
3. pique

Homophones 8 (p. 10)
Answers will vary. Some possible answers listed.
1. quote; verb
2. a place; noun
3. vision; noun/verb
4. a set of rooms in a motel or hotel; noun
5. sugary; adjective

Homophones 9 (p. 10)
Sentences will vary.

Homophones 10 (p. 10)
1. C   2. F   3. A   4. E
5. D   6. B

Homophones 11 (p. 11)
1. horse; hoarse
2. lesson; lessen
3. patients; patience
4. teamed
5. beach; teemed

Homophones 12 (p. 11)
1. ascent – to rise; assent – to agree
2. brake – a device for stopping a vehicle; break – shatter
3. chilly – cold; chili – a type of meaty soup

Homophones 13 (p. 11)
piece – noun; coral – noun; beach – noun

Homophones 14 (p. 11)
1. altar - table
2. course - class

Homophones 15 (p. 11)
Sentences will vary.

Homographs 1 (p. 12)
1. to complete a course of instruction
2. a person who has completed a course of instruction
3. a flat surface
4. argue against

Homographs 2 (p. 12)
Sentences will vary.

Homographs 3 (p. 12)
1. lead
2. carries
3. behavior

Homographs 4 (p. 12)
1. noun
2. adjective
3. verb

Homographs 5 (p. 12)
1. put in order
2. one by one in a line
3. a tool used for smoothing rough edges
4. ordered collection

Homographs 6 (p. 13)
Sentences will vary.

Homographs 7 (p. 13)
1. Verb: attach or fasten
2. Noun: basic supplies

Homographs 8 (p. 13)
1. ad' / dress   2. ad / dress'
3. pre' / sent   4. pre / sent'

Homographs 9 (p. 13)
Definitions will vary.

Homographs 10 (p. 13)
1. ball   2. skate
3. pack   4. shell
5. pack   6. skate
7. ball   8. stamp
9. stamp   10. shell

Synonyms 1 (p. 14)
1. cautious; prudent
2. minor
3. complex; difficult
4. enormous; mammoth
5. scrupulous; detailed; thorough

Synonyms 2 (p. 14)
1. show   2. one
3. knight   4. illness
5. similar

Synonyms 3 (p. 14)
Answers will vary. Possible answers are listed.
1. aggressive; warlike   2. lucky; favorable
3. power; influence   4. relic; ancient
5. exceptional; distinctive

Synonyms 4 (p. 14)
1. E   2. C   3. D   4. B   5. A

Synonyms 5 (p. 14)
Answers will vary. Possible answers are listed.
1. box; container   2. noise; loudness
3. understanding

Antonyms 1 (p. 15)
1. B   2. C   3. D   4. E   5. A

Antonyms 2 (p. 15)
1. aid; assist   2. sincere
3. warlike; hostile   4. speak
5. still; motionless

Antonyms 3 (p. 15)
1. scarce   2. lovable; sweet
3. ignore   4. ugliness
5. normal

Antonyms 4 (p. 15)
Answers will vary. Possible answers are listed.
1. decelerate; brake
2. hesitant; unsure
3. land; sky
4. belittle; revile

Antonyms 5 (p. 15)
1. unreasonable
2. barely
3. ascent; climb
4. inadequate

Compound Words 1 (p. 16)
1. cup/board; card/board; tea/cups; table/spoons
2. red/head; out/standing; work/out; foot/ball

Compound Words 2 (p. 16)
1. a type of snake
2. excess; overflow
3. a measure of power in an engine
4. a key on a keyboard that allows the operator to move backwards one character at a time
5. exclusive rights
6. landing strip; walkway

Compound Words 3 (p. 16)
1. water fall
2. waterfall
3. anybody
4. any body
5. overalls
6. over all

Compound Words 4 (p. 16)
Sentences will vary.

Compound Words 5 (p. 16)
Some possible answers are listed.
1. everyone; everywhere; everything; everyday
2. houseboat; housecoat; houseguest; household; housefly; housekeeper; housewarming; housework
3. weekend; weekday; weeknight; weeklong
4. afterward; afternoon; afterthought; aftertaste; aftershave; afterlife; afterburner
5. backbite; backdrop; backfield; backfire; background; backhand; backlash; backlog; backside; backslide; backspin; backstop; backstretch; backstroke; backtrack; backwash; backwater; backwoods

Compound Words 6 (p. 17)
1. stock/room; how/ever; can/not; white/wash; stair/case; after/noon; paint/brush
2. stout/hearted; swords/man; over/protective; nurse/maid

Compound Words 7 (p. 17)
1. soft ball; softball
2. second hand
3. secondhand

Compound Words 8 (p. 17)
Answers will vary.

Compound Words 9 (p. 17)
Some possible answers are listed.
1. underachieve; underarm; underbelly; underbid; undercarriage; undercharge; underclassman; undercook; undercover; undercurrent; undercut; underdeveloped; underdog; underdone; underestimate; underfed; underfoot; undergo; undergraduate; underground; undergrowth; underhand; underlay; underline; underlying; undermine; undermost; underneath; undernourished; underpass; underpay; underplay; underpowered; underprivileged; underrate; underscore; undersea; undersell; undershirt; underside; undersigned; understaffed; understand; understate; understood; understudy; undertake; undertaking; undertone; undertow; undervalue; underwater; underwear; underweight; underworld; underwrite; underway; underpass
2. daybreak; daydream; daylight; daylily; daylong; daytime; Sunday; birthday; weekday; everyday; workday; someday
3. upbeat; upbringing; upcoming; update; updraft; upend; upgrade; uphill; uphold; upkeep; upland; uplift; upon; upkeep; makeup; backup; checkup; crackup; cutup; holdup; hookup; pinup; roundup; sunup

Compound Words 10 (p. 17)
1. loser; second best; one least likely to win
2. oppressed
3. a glass device filled with sand used to measure time
4. the closest part to the viewer in a painting or photograph
5. dizzy; giddy
6. unbalanced; crooked

© Mark Twain Media, Inc., Publishers

Prefixes 1 (p. 18)
1. unlikely: rare
2. nonprofit: without gain
3. nonsense: silliness
4. untidy: messy

Prefixes 2 (p. 18)
1. illogical   2. immature
3. inactive   4. illiterate
5. irregular

Prefixes 3 (p. 18)
1. T   2. T   3. T   4. T

Prefixes 4 (p. 18)
1. C   2. A   3. B   4. D

Prefixes 5 (p. 18)
Sentences will vary.

Prefixes 6 (p. 19)
1. Answers will vary.
2. *Interstate* means "among two or more states";
   intrastate means "within the same state."

Prefixes 7 (p. 19)
Sentences will vary.

Prefixes 8 (p. 19)
Answers will vary. Some possible words are
listed.
1. transfer; transmit; transport; transcend;
   transcript
2. international; interstate; intermediate;
   intercession; interim
3. subway; subnormal; subtract; subroutine;
   subscript; subterranean

Prefixes 9 (p. 19)
1. F   2. T   3. F   4. T   5. F

Prefixes 10 (p. 19)
Answers will vary.

Suffixes 1 (p. 20)
1. homeless: without a place to live
2. awesome: filled with wonder
3. senseless: without meaning
4. fearsome: scary; fearless: not scared

Suffixes 2 (p. 20)
1. lovable   2. retirement
3. sensible

Suffixes 3 (p. 20)
1. T   2. F   3. F

Suffixes 4 (p. 20)
1. (critic) unflattering; serious
2. (add) more
3. (gradual) slowly
4. (profess) proficient
5. (child) immature
6. (profit) beneficial

Suffixes 5 (p. 20)
Sentences will vary.

Suffixes 6 (p. 21)
Words will vary. Possible answers listed.
1. friendship; courtship
2. avoidance; compliance
3. outlandish; foolish

Suffixes 7 (p. 21)
1. Answers will vary.
2. A *democracy* is a system where the people
   have freedom to elect officials. *Demographic*
   refers to the characteristics of a people in a
   given area.

Suffixes 8 (p. 21)
1. (present) F   2. (select) D
3. (explore) B   4. (appreciate) E
5. (reflect) A   6. (elect) C

Suffixes 9 (p. 21)
Words will vary. Possible answers are listed.
1. freedom; boredom; wisdom; kingdom;
   martyrdom
2. poetic; dramatic; lyric; erratic; epidemic
3. astrology; theology; radiology; cosmetology;
   zoology

Suffixes 10 (p. 21)
1. F   2. F   3. F   4. T   5. F

Prefixes and Suffixes 1 (p. 22)
1. time – instant
2. patient – tolerant
3. perfect – exact
4. happy – glad
5. stop – cease

Prefixes and Suffixes 2 (p. 22)
1. dis- appear -ance
2. im- possible -ility
3. dis- honor -able
4. in- sincere -ity

Prefixes and Suffixes 3 (p. 22)
Sentence will vary.
1. color
2. create
3. content
4. success

Prefixes and Suffixes 4 (p. 22)
Answers may vary. Possible answers given.
1. disconnection
2. mismanagement
3. unfortunately
4. immeasurable
5. disappearance

Prefixes and Suffixes 5 (p. 22)
1. disappointed
2. unmanageable
3. unavoidable

Proper Nouns and Proper Adjectives 1 (p. 23)
1. Czechoslovakian (Czech)
2. Ukrainian
3. Dutch
4. Greek
5. Azerbaijani (Azeri)
6. Finnish

Proper Nouns and Proper Adjectives 2 (p. 23)
1. Hungarians
2. Lithuanians
3. Mozambicans
4. Zimbabweans

Proper Nouns and Proper Adjectives 3 (p. 23)
1. Oklahoma
2. Minnesota
3. Massachusetts
4. Connecticut
5. Mississippi

Proper Nouns and Proper Adjectives 4 (p. 23)
Corrections needed are: Egypt, Lebanon, Kuwait

Proper Nouns and Proper Adjectives 5 (p. 23)
Answers will vary. Check for correct spelling and capitalization.

Numerical Words 1 (p. 24)
1. Quadruplets are four children born at the same time.
2. 5
3. 8
4. 3
5. 5

Numerical Words 2 (p. 24)
1. 1
2. 1
3. 10
4. 2
5. 1,000

Numerical Words 3 (p. 24)
1. 10
2. 100
3. 1,000
4. Once every 200 years
5. Once every 150 years

Numerical Words 4 and 5 (p. 24)
Answers will vary.

Acronyms 1 (p. 25)
1. ID = identification
2. PIN = personal identification number;
   ATM – automated teller machine
3. B & B = bed and breakfast; OJ = orange juice;
   BLT = bacon, lettuce, and tomato;
   PB & J = peanut butter and jelly

Acronyms 2 (p. 25)
1. NIMBY = not in my backyard
2. FYI = for your information
3. ASAP = as soon as possible
4. COD = cash on delivery
5. PC = politically correct or personal computer
6. UPC = universal product code

Acronyms 3 (p. 25)
1. PM = post meridian (after noon)
2. EST = eastern standard time
3. CST = central standard time
4. PST = Pacific standard time
5. AD = Anno Domini ("In the Year of Our Lord")

Acronyms 4 (p. 25)
Sentences will vary.

Acronyms 5 (p. 25)
1. MASH = Mobile Army Surgical Hospital
2. NYPD = New York Police Department
3. PI = private investigator
4. MO = Modus Operandi (method of operation)
5. AKA = also known as
6. SOP = standard operating procedure

© Mark Twain Media, Inc., Publishers

Changing the Part of Speech of Words 1
(p. 26)
1. beautiful   2. foolish
3. personal   4. national
5. stylish   6. musical

Changing the Part of Speech of Words 2
(p. 26)
1. foolishly   2. childishly
3. additionally   4. fractionally
5. truthfully   6. wholly

Changing the Part of Speech of Words 3
(p. 26)
Answers will vary.

Changing the Part of Speech of Words 4
(p. 26)
1. complication   2. collision
3. computer   4. official
5. confidence   6. patron

Changing the Part of Speech of Words 5
(p. 26)
Sentences will vary. One verb form for each word is listed. There are others.
1. introduce   2. confuse
3. arrive   4. entertain

Changing the Part of Speech of Words 6
(p. 27)
Answers will vary.

Changing the Part of Speech of Words 7
(p. 27)
Answers will vary.

Changing the Part of Speech of Words 8
(p. 27)
Sentences will vary. One verb form for each word is listed. There are others.
1. instruct   2. administer
3. abstain   4. multiply
5. know   6. collect

Changing the Part of Speech of Words 9
(p. 27)
Answers will vary.

Changing the Part of Speech of Words 10
(p. 27)
1. permanently   2. obviously
3. gradually   4. secondly
5. practically   6. medically

Words From Mythology 1 (p. 28)
1. sphinx   2. centaur
3. mermaid   4. minotaur

Words From Mythology 2 (p. 28)
1. D   2. C   3. A   4. B

Words From Mythology 3 (p. 28)
1. lion, goat, and serpent-dragon
2. fly   3. 500 years
4. Arabia   5. jinni, djinni

Words From Mythology 4 (p. 28)
1. Roc: from Arabian mythology; a bird large enough to lift and carry an elephant as it flew
2. Cerberus: a three-headed dog with the tail of a lion who guarded the gate to the underworld
3. Selkie: a mythological creature in Irish and Scottish mythology that can transform from a seal to a human by shedding its skin and change back by putting its skin back on
4. Salamander: a mythical reptile that could start fires and live in fire
5. Griffin: a creature with the head and wings of an eagle and body and tail of a lion

Words From Mythology 5 (p. 28)
1. Ireland
2. Egypt
3. India
4. Someone in the house would die.
5.

Classifying Words 1 (p. 29)
These words are mammals: armadillo; echidna; javalina; narwhal; ocelot; pangolin

Classifying Words 2 (p. 29)
These words are not documents: honorarium; jurisdiction; sinecure; tenure

Classifying Words 3 (p. 29)
Fish: flounder; halibut; John Dory; manta ray
Insects: cicada; earwig; praying mantis; walking stick; water strider
Amphibians: hellbender; mud puppy; newt; salamander; yellow-striped caecilian

Classifying Words 4 (p. 29)

1. W	2. L	3. L	4. W
5. W	6. L	7. W	8. W
9. W	10. L		

Classifying Words 5 (p. 29)
Examples will vary.
1. hyperbole: an exaggeration
2. metaphor: a comparison of two unlike items that does not use the words *like* or *as*
3. simile: a comparison of two unlike items using the words *like, as,* or *as if*
4. onomatopoeia: use of a word to imitate a sound

Classifying Words 6 (p. 30)

1. B	2. D	3. C	4. A	5. E

Classifying Words 7 (p. 30)
These words are not birds: barracuda; fibula; marlin; yellow jacket

Classifying Words 8 (p. 30)

1. F	2. C	3. E	4. B
5. D	6. A		

Classifying Words 9 (p. 30)
1. rocks and minerals
2. plants
3. wind
4. weather patterns
5. words and word origins
6. whales

Classifying Words 10 (p. 30)
1. the pound sign (#)
2. the sign ($\sqrt{}$) that means to find the square root
3. the number one followed by 100 zeros
4. a six-pointed star
5. a three-dimensional figure with eight sides
6. an instrument used to measure angles

British English 1 (p. 31)

1. loo	2. coach
3. solicitor	4. whitener
5. chemist	6. busker

British English 2 (p. 31)

1. trunk	2. cookie
3. French fries	4. field

British English 3 (p. 31)
Sentences will vary. Definitions of the words are given.

1. wrench	2. engine muffler
3. truck	4. baby carriage
5. oatmeal	6. trash can

British English 4 (p. 31)

1. B	2. D	3. A	4. F
5. E	6. C		

British English 5 (p. 31)

1. jumble	2. petrol
3. trolley	

Foreign Words and Phrases 1 (p. 32)
Answers will vary. Possible answers are listed.
1. portable; comport; deport; export; import; report; support; transport
2. describe; description; prescribe; prescription; scribble; scriptures; subscribe; subscription; transcribe; transcription
3. eject; inject; interject; project; reject; subject
4. convert; divert; invert; revert; subvert

Foreign Words and Phrases 2 (p. 32)
1. forbidden; prohibited
2. cabbage that has been pickled by soaking in a brine solution
3. a ghostly double or counterpart of a living person
4. a school for young children
5. used to wish someone good health, especially someone who has just sneezed

Foreign Words and Phrases 3 (p. 32)

1. E	2. C	3. B	4. D	5. A

Foreign Words and Phrases 4 (p. 32)
1. hand to hand; one on one in a confrontation or conflict
2. sweet life; the good life
3. the common people

Foreign Words and Phrases 5 (p. 32)
1. chronicle: a story or report told in the order in which events occurred
2. chronic: lasting for a long time; forever
3. chronograph: a stopwatch
4. synchronize: to set watches or clocks to exactly the same time

Latin Phrases 1 (p. 33)
Sentences will vary.

Latin Phrases 2 (p. 33)
1. C   2. D   3. A   4. E   5. B

Latin Phrases 3 (p. 33)
1. *in loco parentis*: in the place of a parent
2. *in medias res*: in the middle of something
3. *in situ*: situated in the original place

Latin Phrases 4 (p. 33)
1. Nothing; *pro bono* means "for the good" or "free of charge."
2. Probably not. It means "an unacceptable or unwelcome person."
3. They were sailing into "unknown territory"; places that had not been mapped.

Latin Phrases 5 (p. 33)
1. It is my fault.
2. Something in exchange for something of equal value
3. I came; I saw; I conquered.

French Phrases 1 (p. 34)
1. useless; unsuccessful
2. Yes; a *bon mot* is a witty remark or comment.
3. No; an *enfant terrible* means a terrible child or an outrageously outspoken or bold person.

French Phrases 2 (p. 34)
1. C   2. D   3. B   4. A

French Phrases 3 (p. 34)
Sentences will vary.

French Phrases 4 (p. 34)
Mark Twain's name was Samuel Clemens.

French Phrases 5 (p. 34)
1. *bon vivant*: a person who lives luxuriously and enjoys good food and drink
2. *cause célèbre*: a widely known controversial case or issue
3. *de rigueur*: strictly required by etiquette, usage, or fashion
4. *fait accompli*: an accomplished fact, presumably irreversible
5. *je ne sais quoi*: I know not what; an elusive quality
6. *carte blanche*: unrestricted power to act on one's own

Idioms 1 (p. 35)
1. goes against my grain
2. on cloud nine
3. all thumbs
4. cut the mustard
5. out on a limb

Idioms 2 (p. 35)
1. anything is possible; unlimited
2. very confusing
3. work until late at night; work long hours

Idioms 3 (p. 35)
1. C   2. D   3. E   4. A   5. B

Idioms 4 (p. 35)
1. D   2. A   3. E   4. C   5. B

Idioms 5 (p. 35)
Sentences will vary.

Idioms 6 (p. 36)
Sentences will vary.

Idioms 7 (p. 36)
1. C   2. D   3. B   4. A   5. E

Idioms 8 (p. 36)
Answers will vary
1. reveal a secret; say something wrong
2. hard work
3. hurry
4. make a good impression
5. attempting something too difficult or dangerous
6. say something embarrassing

Idioms 9 (p. 36)
Answers will vary.

Idioms 10 (p. 36)
1. cover
2. blue
3. wrist
4. hand
5. mountain